Kenne

UNSOLVED MYSTERIES

It's amazing that even today, with all the ultra high-tech scientific equipment available to us, there are still phenomena that cannot be satisfactorily explained.

Do extra-terrestrial beings really exist? Is it possible to create a perpetual motion machine? Why and how have some people, for no apparent reason, suddenly disappeared without trace? Is there really a creature lurking in the depths of Loch Ness?

These and many more questions have continued to puzzle and fascinate mankind, who has never been able to find credible answers to the world's intriguing mysteries.

Kenneth Ireland

UNSOLVED MYSTERIES

Hippo Books
Scholastic Publications Limited
London

Scholastic Publications Ltd.,
10 Earlham Street, London WC2H 9RX, UK

Scholastic Inc.,
730 Broadway, New York, NY 10003, USA

Scholastic Tab Publications Ltd.,
123 Newkirk Road, Richmond Hill,
Ontario L4C 3G5, Canada

Ashton Scholastic Pty. Ltd.,
P O Box 579, Gosford, New South Wales,
Australia

Ashton Scholastic Ltd.,
165 Marua Road, Panmure, Auckland 6,
New Zealand

First published by Scholastic Publications Ltd., 1988

Copyright © Kenneth Ireland, 1988

ISBN 0 590 70993 3

All rights reserved

Made and printed by
Cox and Wyman Ltd., Reading, Berks.

Typeset in Plantin by
COLLAGE (Design in Print)
Longfield Hill, Kent.

This book is sold subject to the condition that it shall not, by way of trade or otherwise be lent, resold, hired out, or otherwise circulated without the publisher's prior consent in any form of binding or cover other than that in which it is published and without a similar condition, including this condition, being imposed upon the subsequent purchaser.

Contents

The Orphyreus wheel

He called himself Orphyreus. Even that wasn't his real name, but that's only the beginning of the mystery. Nobody knows where he came from, or where he went afterwards. All we know for certain is that in 1717 he was thirty-six years old, that he was German, that he was uncouth and penniless, and that he was described as "a shaggy giant with long black hair and wild eyes". That was when he arrived at Hesse-Cassell, in Germany, ruled by Prince Karl, known as the Landgrave of Hesse.

He was put into the castle dungeons for being drunk, but when he was brought before the Landgrave the next morning for sentence, he claimed he could invent a perpetual motion machine — one which would never need fuel or power because it would keep going by itself.

He was so convincing that Prince Karl, instead of sentencing him, talked with him for the whole morning, gave him clothes and a workshop and even made him a town councillor.

There was one good reason why Prince Karl believed him. Orphyreus had already invented three such machines, but the Church authorities had accused him of being in league with the devil and, because of his activities, he had already been deported from half a dozen different countries in Europe and his machines had been destroyed.

When the machine was finished, it consisted of a drum or wheel which was twelve feet high and two feet wide. An axle through the centre pivoted on two wooden uprights. At the top of each of those uprights was a wooden cross-piece or rocker from which hung a pendulum. The huge drum had a wooden frame, but the outer covering was simply oiled cloth.

It stood in a large chamber on the ground floor of the castle. A heavy, iron-bound door was the only entrance, there were no windows, and the walls were four feet thick. Two scientists came to inspect the invention at Prince Karl's request — Baron Fischer, architect to the Emperor of Austria, and Professor s'Gravesande of Leiden University in Holland, who was also a great friend of Sir Isaac Newton, the famous British scientist and mathematician.

They were astonished. Many people had tried to make a perpetual motion machine, but had failed — because such a thing is scientifically impossible. Each of them had exposed several previous frauds but this machine actually worked! It would raise beams, pump water or drive mills, and all without using any fuel and it ran at a steady twenty-six revolutions per minute (the Baron timed it on his pocket-watch).

However, Orphyreus wouldn't let them see the mechanism inside the wheel "until my work has been paid for". That was suspicious. It was just possible that there was a man inside operating it. So the two scientists had the room sealed, with the machine working inside it, no way in or out, and the room remained sealed for eight weeks, from 12th November, 1717, to 4th January, 1718.

When, without warning, they unsealed the room on that day, the wheel was still working exactly as when they had left it! No one could have remained alive inside that sealed room all that time, and they had already examined it carefully to make sure there was no other way in or out. The scientists were convinced.

The price Orphyreus demanded for his invention was twenty thousand English pounds, an enormous sum of money in those days. But with such a machine, anyone who owned it, and was able to make more machines like it, would make a fortune. It was worth the money and the professor said he would write at once to Holland, and to Sir Isaac Newton in London, to raise that tremendous sum.

We don't know what caused Orphyreus to go into a rage shortly afterwards, but in the middle of the night a few days later, he took an axe and smashed the wheel to pieces. When the guards arrived to find the cause of the noise, together with Prince Karl and the two scientists in their night clothes, Orphyreus ran shouting out of the castle and into the nearby woods. Search parties were sent out to find him but he seemed to have disappeared. And, although Prince Karl warned the authorities throughout Europe to be on the watch for him and bring him back, Orphyreus was never found, nor ever seen or heard of again.

The wheel was completely smashed. From the wreckage and splintered wood there was no way of finding out how it had worked, nor how to rebuild its mechanism. Its inventor had utterly destroyed it.

Orphyreus was undoubtedly a madman — and a genius. He could not have used clockwork inside his wheel — for one thing, no clockwork mechanism could have provided such fast acceleration nor kept the wheel moving for eight weeks non-stop. It could not have worked on some magnetic principle, and electric motors had not been invented. It must have used some mechanical method.

But what? Dozens of attempts have since been made to solve the mystery of the "Orphyreus Wheel" — and all have failed. It all ought to have been impossible.

If Orphyreus had not been insane, the Industrial Revolution would have arrived a century earlier than it actually did, and instead of using steam engines, the driving force could have been versions of the Orphyreus machine needing no fuel of any sort.

The whole of modern industry might have been changed. Over two hundred and fifty years later we still don't know who Orphyreus really was, what happened to him, nor, most importantly, how his machine worked.

The theory of the "over-balancing wheel" has been suggested to explain the working of the Orphyreus wheel. If weights which are attached to a wheel keep falling in order to make the wheel turn, then the wheel will move, but only until the wheel becomes balanced and then it will invariably stop. That's bound to happen, but Orphyreus's wheel didn't stop!

People who catch fire

In 1763, all that could be found of the Countess di Bandi was a heap of ashes and her legs, which, with her stockings, were quite untouched. Soot was floating around in her bedroom, and a couple of candles had vanished — except for their wicks. Otherwise there was no damage in the room.

In 1835, Professor James Hamilton of Nashville University, USA, noticed to his horror that a flame was coming out of the skin on his left leg. Slapping at it had no effect, so he put his hand over the flame instead, and it disappeared.

In 1851, a house-painter in Paris foolishly bet that he would eat a lighted candle. As soon as he started to eat it, a blue flame appeared at his lips. Neither he nor his friends could put out the flame, and, in half an hour, his head and chest were burned to carbon. The fire didn't stop until he was just a heap of ashes.

In 1880, while a Dr Hartwell was attending a woman patient at Ayer, Massachusetts, USA, flames suddenly burst out of her body and legs and she died in a horrific blaze.

In 1919, the body of J Temple Thurston, a well-known author, was found horribly burned from the waist down. There was no sign of fire in the room, the rest of his body was untouched, and his clothes weren't even scorched where the fire had been.

This peculiar — and fortunately rare — mysterious happening is known as *spontaneous human combustion*. And it's happened to all sorts of people. Frequently, only the body is damaged, not the clothes nor the surroundings. For instance, in 1922, a woman from Sydenham, Kent, a Mrs Euphemia Johnson, was burned to blackened bones but her clothes were totally undamaged.

On the other hand, it sometimes happens differently. Phyllis Newcombe was aged twenty-two. As she left a dance hall in Chelmsford, Essex, in 1938, she was suddenly engulfed in blue flames, and, together with her clothes, turned to ashes within minutes. Something similar happened to Mrs Mary Carpenter, also in 1938. She burst into flames while holidaying on a hired boat on the Norfolk Broads. She was completely reduced to ashes while her husband and children watched, unable to help. Both they and the boat were unharmed and undamaged.

And, when Mrs Mary Reeser, of St Petersburg, Florida, USA, was incinerated to ashes while sitting in an armchair on 2nd July, 1951 — the chair was reduced to some coiled springs, a lamp next to the chair was reduced to just its metal frame, plastic kitchen utensils had melted — yet a newspaper on the floor near the chair wasn't even charred. One of Mrs Reeser's feet also remained unburned.

It has been estimated that the temperature necessary to reduce a body to ashes has to be *at least* 1500°C. Even in a crematorium, after twelve hours at that temperature, bones never disappear completely. They shatter into tiny fragments — never just soft ash!

One of the most famous recent cases involved Dr John Bentley, who lived at 403 North Main Street, Coudersport, Pennsylvania, USA, and it happened on 5th December, 1966. The heat produced burned through the floor to leave a thirty-five centimetre high cone of ashes in the basement below. When the rest of the body was found upstairs, there was just one foot and a slipper quite undamaged. A bath-tub nearby was blackened but the paint was not even blistered.

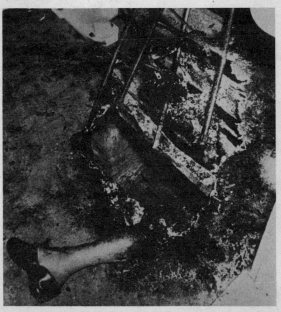

The remains of Dr John Bentley, 1966

In the same year, Billy Peterson was in his parked car in Detroit, USA when flames were seen to burst from his body. The heat was so intense that the dashboard of the car melted. But when they got him out, although his body was completely charred, his clothes were not even singed!

Explanation for any of this? None! But at least two dozen cases of spontaneous human combustion are known. It is thought that there *might* be some connection with the strength of the earth's magnetic field at the time, but that is not certain.

Only two people who have burst into flames have not died at once. One was Professor Hamilton who managed to put the fire out. The other was Madge Knight who burst into flames on 18th November, 1943. She didn't die at once, but died of her injuries on 6th December. She was severely burned in bed — but the sheets on which she was lying weren't even scorched.

So far, it's not only a complete mystery but it ought to be something which is quite impossible — but it isn't!

The Indian rope trick

This has been performed out of doors in full view of hundreds of people, and, what's more, it has been photographed at the time. But there's something odd about it which has never been properly explained — and the few people who have performed it aren't going to tell, of course.

An Indian fakir, or holy man, accompanied by a boy, appears in front of the crowd with a long rope. He coils the rope and lays it on the ground and the boy stands beside it. The fakir then throws the rope into the air — and it remains there. The boy then climbs the rope — and disappears. The boy then appears again at the top of the rope, climbs down it, the fakir pulls the rope down and coils it again, and the trick is over.

On a theatre stage, a similar trick can be performed using concealed wires and such, but this famous trick has been performed in India, in the open air, where it would be impossible for hidden wires to be used.

On one occasion, a spectator actually took a photograph while the trick was taking place. When the photograph was developed, it showed that the fakir, the boy and the coiled rope were all on the ground, but the spectator had been quite convinced that, at the time when he had taken the photograph, he was seeing the boy half-way up the rope which was supporting itself on nothing!

Could it be that in some way the fakir hypnotizes an entire audience to make them see what is not really there but what the fakir wants them to think is happening? No one knows at the moment, apart from the few fakirs who have managed to perform the trick, and they won't say!

But we do have two strange *levitations*, as rising into the air is called, recorded on film. One was that of Subbayah Pullavar in India in 1936, and the other that of Nana Owuku in Togo, Africa, in May, 1975. Actual photographs of the levitation by Subbayah Pullavar were printed in the *Illustrated London News* on 6th June, 1936.

The levitation by Subbayah Pullavar, 1936

In front of about a hundred and fifty people, Subbayah went into a small tent. After a few minutes, the tent was removed and there was Subbayah floating in the air "with no support whatsoever except for resting one hand lightly on top of a cloth-covered stick". After about four minutes, the tent was put back in place so that he could return to the ground while hidden from view.

The point was that the person who took the photographs, P T Plunkett, was close enough to be able to see through the thin walls of the tent at the end of the performance. He said that Subbayah seemed to sway, then very slowly descend to the ground, still in the horizontal position, taking about five minutes over it. The stick was about three feet tall. Plunkett, together with several other planters living in India, saw the event several times and they were all quite convinced that no trickery was involved.

Perhaps. But the fact that Subbayah felt he had to be hidden inside a tent at the beginning and at the end of the performance might indicate otherwise. After all, this is the sort of thing which can be performed on a theatre stage, and that definitely involves trickery. But if Plunkett really did see what he says he saw inside that tent . . .

There is one other example which seems to show that levitation really happened without trickery, but unfortunately there are no photographs. In the 1950s John Keel was at Sikkim. He met a Tibetan monk and asked him whether this sort of thing was possible.

The old lama, or monk, struggled to his feet, pressed one hand on top of his stick, then, to Keel's astonishment, slowly lifted his legs from the ground until he was sitting *cross-legged in the air*. There was apparently nothing behind him, or under him, and his only support was the stick which the lama seemed to be using just to keep his balance. Then he slowly lowered himself to the ground again.

He had, said John Keel, proved his point!

The flying friar

St Joseph of Copertino was very odd indeed. What happened to him would be unbelievable, or at least would be regarded as sheer exaggeration, but for the fact that those who had actually seen him do it at various times had included the Pope, Prince Leopold of Tuscany, Princess Maria of Savoy, the King of Poland — Casimir V, together with dozens of monks, nuns and ordinary people.

St Joseph was born in 1603 and didn't seem to be very bright. In fact, at school he was nicknamed "Open Mouth" because he used to sit with his mouth open. At the age of eight he became strongly religious and built a little altar for himself at home. By the time he was twelve he had begun to torture himself as a penance for his "sins".

He tried to become a friar when he was seventeen, but two of his uncles were already friars and made sure he was turned down. He was, they said, much too ignorant to become either a friar or a monk.

Eventually, though, he did become a friar near Copertino, and promptly added to his penances, going barefoot all the time and sleeping on plain wooden boards instead of a bed. And, when he was at last accepted as a full friar, on 28th March, 1628, he started whipping himself with a whip which had pins and star-shaped pieces of iron fastened to its thongs as well. He was ordered to stop when blood was found splattered over the walls of his cell!

Then rumours began about the strange powers which this very odd monk seemed to have. What was worse, the other monks were fairly sure that these powers didn't come from heaven! As a result he was sent to be investigated by the church authorities in Naples.

While he was there, he went to Mass in the church and suddenly rose into the air and flew over the rest of the congregation. A group of nuns from St Ligorio were alarmed, thinking that he might set his clothes on fire when his robes passed over the lighted candles. The church authorities, equally alarmed, sent him to Rome to see Pope Urban VIII.

As he entered the room where the Pope sat, he rose into the air and, to the Pope's astonishment, remained there for at least a minute before floating down to the floor again.

The Pope sent him to be a friar at Assissi and, from then on, every time Joseph felt delighted about something, he would begin to "fly". Once he drifted upwards in church and then glided the full length of the church to land on the altar — without stopping.

Prince Leopold of Tuscany once saw him, kneeling in prayer, alone in a chapel, suddenly float upwards still in a kneeling position. The Duke of Brunswick didn't believe a word of it, so he arranged to watch Joseph in secret in February, 1651, from a private staircase to the Chapel of Noviziato Vecchio, accompanied by two friends and the Superior of the monks.

While all four of them watched, unknown to Joseph, Joseph rose into the air, moved backwards about five yards, then returned to his original position. The Duke of Brunswick was not a Roman Catholic, but a Lutheran. He was so astonished that he became a Roman Catholic as a result of this!

Joseph died on 18th September, 1663.

Now, even if we ignore all the unlikely tales told about him, such as those which originated years after Joseph's death, and which were almost certainly exaggerations, we still have some totally inexplicable events. There was no way in which Joseph could have used trickery. Joseph was *not* very clever, and was more than a little odd, even if later he was declared to be a saint. He would not have been capable of devising tricks of this kind, especially one involving entering a room where he had never been before to go into the presence of the Pope. And, during his lifetime, even the most sceptical became convinced of Joseph's ability to defy gravity.

But he was not the only person to have done this sort of thing. St Teresa of Avilon was another. Joseph of Copertino never described what rising into the air felt like, but St Teresa did. She wrote: "It seemed to me, when I tried to make some resistance, as if a great force beneath my feet lifted me up . . . . I confess it threw me into a great fear, very great indeed at first . . . ".

She was, in fact, scared every time it happened to her!

Daniel Dunglas Home

Daniel Dunglas Home was an American who was invited to the home of Ward Cheney in Connecticut in August, 1852, at the age of nineteen.

Daniel Dunglas Home

While he was there, to everyone's astonishment, including apparently his own, he suddenly floated up into the air and then came down again. Then he did it again. And the third time it happened, his head and hands were pressed against the ceiling of the room.

That he actually did this was vouched for by everyone present, but one of those in the house was F L Burr, newspaper reporter for the *Hartford Times*. He wasn't going to miss such an amazing scoop, and promptly wrote an account for his newspaper of what had happened.

Of course, trickery was at once suspected, although how he could have managed to rig up the trick in somebody else's house no one was sure. But then he managed to repeat the event in all sorts of places and at various times, and those who saw him do it included William Makepeace Thackery, the famous Victorian novelist who wrote *Vanity Fair*; John Ruskin, the famous art critic of the time; Mark Twain, the famous American humorist who wrote *Tom Sawyer*; and Emperor Napoleon III of France.

In addition, Home could apparently make heavy objects float into the air as well. Once a heavy table first tilted and then rose from the carpet, while the ornaments on top stayed put. On another occasion this even happened to a grand piano. Objects such as bamboo tables, which were not very heavy, had been made to move by "mediums" before, but never had anything like this been seen! And this sort of thing took place in people's houses, not on a carefully prepared stage in a theatre.

What made Daniel Dunglas Home unique was that he continued to levitate for about forty years, including occasions in broad daylight and when he was totally surrounded by people.

Harry Houdini, the escapologist and conjurer, saw him perform once, and claimed he could reproduce everything which Home did — but never managed to. Not once could anyone find the slightest evidence of fraud or trickery to explain his ability to rise into the air, despite every possible test.

Sir William Crookes, later the President of the British Association for the Advancement of Science, saw him perform in 1871, and what he wrote was this:

"The phenomena I am prepared to attest are so extraordinary, and so directly opposed to the most firmly rooted articles of scientific belief that even now, on recalling the details of what I witnessed, there is an antagonism in my mind between *reason*, which pronounced it to be scientifically impossible, and the consciousness that my senses, both of sight and touch, are not lying witnesses."

That is to say that what Sir William saw was scientifically impossible, but there is no doubt that he saw it happen. What we also know is that Sir William actually touched Home while he was rising into the air — almost certainly to find the hidden wires or other tricks which Home was using. There weren't any.

Home, like St Teresa of Avilon, also wrote how it felt. He said:

"I feel no hands supporting me, and, since the first time, I have never felt fear; though, should I have fallen from the ceiling of some of the rooms in which I have been raised, I could not have escaped serious injury. I am generally lifted up perpendicularly. My arms frequently become rigid, and are drawn above my head, as if I were grasping the unseen power which slowly raises me from the floor."

If Home were performing a trick, nobody who ever saw him could discover any way in which it could be done, and that included some of the foremost scientists of his time. To the end of his life Home himself claimed that there was no trick — he simply discovered that it was something that he was able to do. And, as his own account shows, at first it seemed to have taken him as much by surprise as it did everyone else.

We still have an amazing mystery which has never been solved. One interesting question might be, of course — why hasn't it happened to more people? Supposing it suddenly happened to you . . .

The Loch Ness monster

Is there one? Well, it certainly seems like it! In AD 565 St Columba was travelling to Inverness with his companions. He had told one of them to swim out into the gloomy loch, or lake, to bring back a boat which had drifted away. While the man was in the water, a "strange

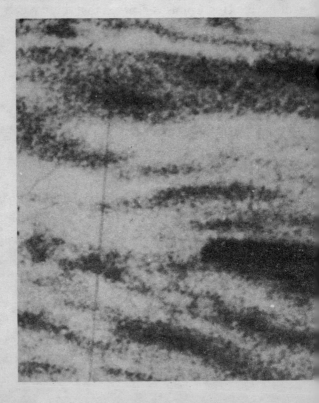

beast" rose out of the loch just in front of the swimmer. St Columba saw it, shouted at it, and it submerged again.

Since then there have been more than three thousand "sightings" of the mysterious creature in Loch Ness. Most of the modern sightings date from 1933 onwards, but that's because in that year a new road was built along

Robert Wilson's photograph of the Loch Ness Monster, 1934

the north shore of the loch, giving a much clearer view across the water. The first people to see it from the new road were Mr and Mrs John Mackay on 14th April, 1933.

In November, 1933, the first photograph was taken by Hugh Grey, an engineer who lived in the village of Floyers, on the south side of the loch. The creature was, he said, about forty feet (about twelve metres) long. When people suggested that he had faked the photograph, he sent it to Kodak, the film manufacturers. They declared there was no doubt that the photograph was perfectly genuine.

This photograph, however, was too vague to give clear details, but then, in April, 1934, Robert Wilson, a London surgeon, parked at Invermoriston, and at once a small head on a long neck came up out of the water. Wilson dashed back to his car, grabbed his camera and took a series of photographs which also revealed part of a large body underneath the water.

Hundreds of photographs have since been taken, but of course some have not been genuine. When people expect to see a mysterious monster, they begin to think that anything which comes up out of the water must be it! Consequently, some of the photographs have quite obviously been of such things as floating tree trunks and even upturned boats.

In 1960, Tim Dinsdale, an aero-engineer, actually managed to take a four-minute movie film of the monster. He also studied a hundred genuine eye-witness accounts dating from 1933 to 1958, because he wanted to find what details were identical in all of them.

All the accounts varied a little, but every one mentioned a small head on the end of a neck. The length of the neck was estimated to be from one-and-a-half metres to "long and undulating". Also, the head was always described as like that of a reptile. The body was always described as vast, always dark in colour, and either a series of humps or "like a whale".

The tail was powerful, but there weren't enough details to decide exactly how big. But, when the creature moved forward, the water was disturbed twenty feet, or about six metres, behind the body. The speed was always described as "rapid".

It had been seen to dive head first, followed by the neck and then the body, when it was startled, but otherwise just seemed to sink straight down into the water.

In 1981, there was a full-scale expedition, approved by the Scientific Exploration Society, to find out what could be there. They used underwater photography and sonar — the sound-detecting apparatus which locates and identifies objects under water. The monster was not found, but what was discovered were some "shrimps" which couldn't be identified by the British Museum's Natural History Department, because until then their existence had been unknown.

So, for the next year's expedition, the Goodyear airship was brought in to assist by also searching from the air. On 7th June, 1982, sonar contact was made with an unknown object which was moving between fourteen and eighteen metres below the surface —

unfortunately too deep in those murky waters for anything to be visible from the air. Whatever it was then moved off quickly, but in that year thirteen sonar contacts were made, and they still failed to find exactly what was the cause. The only certainty was that it was something which *moved*.

In 1987 the most recent investigation took place. Again, sonar picked up "something", at great depth this time, which was certainly *not* something lying naturally on the bed of the loch. Had it been just that, the sonar equipment would have been able to identify it.

There is definitely something there. Bernard Heuvelmanns, the Belgian zoologist, examined five hundred and eighty-seven reports of sightings of the monster dating from 1639 to 1964. After he had eliminated all the obvious hoaxes, and also all accounts which were too vague to be of much use, or which were in any way doubtful, he found himself still left with no fewer than three hundred and fifty-eight sightings during that period which were genuine *beyond all doubt*.

So what could it be? At one time Loch Ness was connected to the sea. Could it be that some large sea creatures, possibly sea mammals, were trapped there, and have been breeding ever since? If so, there could be more than one monster at a time, and the two descriptions of "humped" and "like a whale" would seem to indicate that as well. There would certainly be enough food in the loch for a few of creatures like these to eat.

A possibility which has been suggested is that

it could be a gigantic eel. This is doubtful, though some eels have been known to grow more than a foot thick, and long in proprtion. It could be a giant sturgeon. One which was eleven feet long (nearly three and a half metres) was caught in the 1960s off the coast of Wales, and far bigger ones are not unknown. But, again, it's doubtful.

What has to be remembered, too, is the famous mistake made by Baron Cuvier in 1812. He was a world-famous naturalist, who in that year announced: "There is little hope of discovering a new species of large quadruped." Almost at once the tapir was discovered, previously unknown, together with many more previously unknown animals.

And the coelocanth, a very curious-looking fish, had been extinct for thousands of years. Only fossils of it had been found anywhere in the world — until it suddenly turned up, quite obviously alive and well, in 1952. Since then dozens have been found. It's just that we didn't realize that it still existed!

So — there's *something* in Loch Ness. Far too many reports, sightings and photographs of it have appeared for the fact to be otherwise. But, as for what it is, or how it got there — that is one of the great mysteries which remain so far unsolved.

Other water monsters

Loch Ness isn't the only Scottish Loch to have a monster in it. Loch Morar might also have one. This loch is also in the county of Inverness, but near the west coast between two stretches of land called North Morar and South Morar. The Loch Morar monster is known as Morag.

One of the most recent sightings happened in June, 1976. A woman who had lived near the loch for fourteen years was gardening about two hundred metres away from the shore. Suddenly she heard a splash in the water, and, about two hundred metres into the loch, she saw a big, dark hump raised out of the water. She said it seemed to be about a metre high.

She called her children to come and look as well. While they were all watching, the "thing" submerged, surfaced again, then began to move about, "as if it were trying to catch fish". Then it headed off up the loch, leaving a big wake of disturbed water behind it, before finally disappearing.

Colonel Bashford-Snell and Tim Dinsdale, who were on an expedition nearby at the time, heard about the sighting and went to see her about it. She described it as looking more like a whale than anything else and her children agreed.

So, could it really have been the monster, Morag, which they had seen — and if so, what sort of monster was it?

Such creatures are not only found in Scottish lochs, either. In 1861 an absolutely enormous giant squid was caught a hundred and twenty

Illustration of the giant squid caught in 1861

miles north-east of Tenerife. In 1881, a Scottish fishing boat, the *Bertie*, was actually attacked by a creature, a humped one this time, which almost managed to capsize it. Although shots were fired at it, the creature carried on diving around the boat for several hours before moving off. And, before then, on 6th August, 1848, Captain McQuhae, and several of the crew of *HMS Daedalus*, saw a dark head with a shaggy mane down its long neck watching them off the coast of West Africa. In his report, Captain McQuhae estimated the legnth of the creature as "at least sixty feet".

And, in 1964, a team from Moscow University, Russia, reported seeing a creature in Lake Khaiyre, in Siberia, which looked suspiciously like a *dinosaur*. They simply couldn't identify it as a known species at all.

In 1966, John Ridgeway and Chay Blyth were rowing a boat across the Atlantic. They were the first people to do that. One night John Ridgeway was rowing when he saw the shape of a mysterious creature about thirty-five feet long (about ten and a half metres) coming towards the boat — fast. Then it disappeared beneath them and was not seen again.

Both Ridgeway and Blyth, of course, knew what whales, sharks, dolphins and porpoises looked like. This creature was certainly nothing like one of those. It was a type that Ridgeway had never seen in his life before, and what made it stand out so clearly, apart from the fact that the night was not absolutely dark, was the phosphorescence which surrounded it as it rose from the sea and then dropped back again —

plus its enormous size and fast speed.

One "gigantic beast, seventy feet long with jaws four feet wide" was once actually taken by surprise. A diver called Robert Le Serer, diving on the Great Barrier Reef of Australia, was alarmed to find it lying on the sea-bed in front of him!

In the past, sailors' tales of "sea serpents" were regarded as being tall stories. It seems now that they were not always the total exaggerations which everyone thought!

The Flannan lighthouse keepers

The Flannan Isles are in the Outer Hebrides, off the coast of Scotland, and lie west of the Isle of Lewis. There were four keepers of the Eilean Mor lighthouse on the Flannan Isles, but one of them, Joseph Moore, spent Christmas night, in the year 1900, on shore.

The Flannan lighthouse

He should have been on duty, but the weather had been too bad and the seas too rough for the relief ship, the *Hesperus*, to take him to the lighthouse. It had been like that for several days. Also what was worse was that, for several days, no light had been seen from the lamp set two hundred and seventy-five feet above sea-level, and that light was so powerful that it should have been visible for forty miles!

The lighthouse took four years to build, on a site near the ruined chapel of St Flannan on an island only five hundred yards long by two hundred yards wide (four hundred and fifty-seven metres by a hundred and eighty-three metres). It had been completed in December, 1899, so in 1900 it had been operating for just one year.

There were two landing stages on the island, one on the east and one on the west, so that, if the sea was rough on one side, there was always a chance that a boat could land on the other. And, in the lighthouse at that moment, there should have been the other three keepers — James Ducat, Donald MacArthur, and Thomas Marshall who was in charge.

The *Hesperus*, now with Joseph Moore on board, finally managed to put to sea on Boxing Day, 1900. The seas were still very rough. The ship arrived near the eastern landing stage, which had zigzag steps cut into the rock above it, but there were no answering flags in reply to the ship's signals. However, a rowing boat was put out and this managed to land.

The lighthouse was completely deserted. The fire in the fireplace had gone out. The clock had stopped. And, of course, the lamp had been allowed to go out. Otherwise everything was as it should have been. Except — the three lighthouse keepers were nowhere on the island.

The men returned to the lighthouse and examined the log which Thomas Marshall had to keep, writing everything in it that happened while they were on duty.

The entries in the book recorded very high waves "tearing at the lighthouse" and saying they had never seen such a storm before. It was so bad that they had all prayed, especially on 13th December. There was no entry for 14th December, but the final entry, written at nine o'clock on the morning of 15th December, read: "Storm ended, sea calm. God is over all."

Two items were missing — the sea-boots and oilskins belonging to Thomas Marshall and James Ducat. On the west landing stage were signs of storm damage. A crane stood there, sixty-five feet above the water. That was all right, but, wrapped round it, was a tangle of rope.

They knew the rope came from a tool chest which was kept another forty feet higher up the rock from the crane, but then they found that chest missing as well. So that had been washed away by a wave which must have risen to a height of a hundred and ten feet, or thirty-three and a half metres!

At first it seemed obvious that the three men had been washed away by this tremendous wave, but then it was found that this wasn't true. According to the lighthouse log the sea had been calm on 15th December. What's more, a steamship, the *SS Archer*, had passed near the lighthouse about midnight on 15th December, had reported that it was a "comparatively calm day" — and had noted that the light was out then. So, whatever had happened, it had happened on 15th December, 1900.

The three men were never seen again. No bodies, nor any items of clothing or equipment belonging to them, were ever washed ashore, anywhere. They had just — disappeared, as if into thin air.

No one has ever solved the mystery for certain. All sorts of explanations have been made, however. Supposing the keepers had gone to the landing stage in calm weather, but one of them had slipped into the sea and the other two had drowned trying to rescue him? But the platform was littered with ropes and lifebelts. Experienced keepers would have used them instead of jumping in after the victim.

Another suggestion — one of them had gone mad, killed the other two, then committed suicide himself. But that couldn't be true, because no weapons were missing.

What complicated the mystery was that the local people of the Outer Hebrides regarded the Flannan Islands, also known as the Seven Hunters, as haunted. Farmers actually kept sheep on the islands, but while they would sail there in daylight, in calm weather, to look after them, not a single farmer would ever dare to set foot on the islands if there was any risk they might have to remain there overnight. There were stories of many peculiar things that had happened to people who had dared stay there in the dark!

There is only one possible solution, and it took forty-seven years before it was suggested, and even this is not entirely certain.

In 1947, Iain Campbell, a Scottish journalist, was standing near the west landing stage, looking down at it. It was a calm day. Suddenly, without any warning, the sea rose "about seventy feet" with amazing suddenness and washed over the steps and the concrete platform "as if there had been an earthquake on the sea bed," he reported.

Anyone who had been standing on the platform, the steps, or the lower path, would have been washed away. There was no warning that this was going to happen, and no sound as the sea came up.

The whole thing lasted for about a minute, then the sea subsided again. It had never been known before, and doesn't seem to have happened since. So, *if* this was what happened on 15th December, in the year 1900, we do have a possible solution.

Since the storm seemed to have ended, James Ducat and Thomas Marshall might have put on their sea-boots and oilskins to protect them from the icy spray and gone down to do some work on the lower part of the west landing stage.

Then Donald MacArthur, in his ordinary clothes, could have wandered down to the crane platform after them. If there had been a similar freak tide, like the one which Iain Campbell had seen, all three could have been swept to their deaths.

But, if that's not what happened, we still have no sensible explanation.

The Mary Celeste

What happened on board the *Mary Celeste* is perhaps the most famous sea mystery of all time. When it was first reported, it was so strange that the ship was even referred to as the *Marie Celeste*, because *Mary* seemed too ordinary a name for such a strange event.

The facts are these. The ship left New York harbour on 4th November, 1872. It was carrying a cargo of crude alcohol for Genoa, Italy, and on board was the Captain, Benjamin Briggs, his wife, Sarah, and their two-year-old daughter, Sophia. The name of the first mate was Albert Richardson.

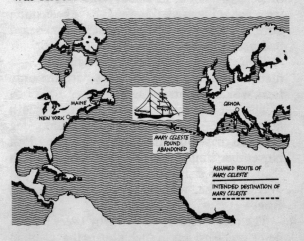

The route of the *Mary Celeste*, 1872

Thirty days later it was found totally deserted, but still sailing on course. Captain Morehouse, of the *Dei Gratia* which found her, said that, from the way the sails were set before they boarded her, it was impossible that the ship could have kept that course with the sails set that way.

When they got on board the *Mary Celeste*, they found that breakfast had been left half-eaten. Mrs Brigg's sewing machine was on a table. Washing hung drying on a line in the crew's quarters, and clothes lay, completely dry and undisturbed, on the ship's bunks. On a table, there was an open bottle of cough medicine which had not spilled at all, showing that the ship had not been caught in a storm.

Down in the bottom of the ship, in the bilges, there were three feet of water. But that didn't mean the ship had started to sink at any time. Since it was built of wood, while the pumps were not being used, this would have been quite normal. One of the ten casks of alcohol on board had been opened.

There is just one other significant fact — a lifeboat was missing. And these are the only facts which anyone really knows.

The weather had been stormy on 24th November — the entry in the ship's log reported it. But the entry for the 25th November simply noted the direction in which the ship was sailing, so by then the storm was over. And that was the last item that Captain Briggs ever wrote.

The real mystery, then, is why every human being on board left in such a hurry that Captain

Briggs had even sliced the top off his boiled egg and then left it uneaten. Perhaps the opened cask of alcohol might suggest an answer — a risk of fire, so that, as a precaution, everyone left the ship in the missing lifeboat until they discovered whether the ship was going to explode or not. But there was no sign of any fire. And, if they had left for that reason, why had they not all returned when they had found that it was perfectly safe?

There couldn't have been a mutiny by the ship's crew. If there's a mutiny, the mutineers don't go off in the same boat as their victims, they send them off and then stay on board!

There are two mysteries, in fact: why they all left the ship in the first place, and why none of the people on board were never seen again, either alive or dead.

We don't know what happened, or why it happened, but, whatever it was, it took place on 25th November, 1872.

The crew who died

The *Mary Celeste* mystery might be the most famous one connected with ships at sea, but there is a much less well-known mystery which is much more amazing, and baffling. Because, in this case, no one disappeared. They were all found — but they were all dead! And nobody knows why.

In February, 1948, the Dutch freighter, the *Ourang Medan*, was sailing through the Straits of Malacca on its way to Djakarta, which is in Java. Suddenly it sent out a "May Day" message on its radio, indicating an urgent emergency. The message was most surprising. It was to the effect that the Captain and all the officers were already dead, the entire crew were either dead or dying, and that the one sending the message himself was also "near death".

Unfortunately, although quite a number of ships within radio range picked up the signal, for some reason the radio operator was not able to give the exact position of the *Ourang Medan*. Nevertheless, within three hours, one of the other ships had found it with sharks cruising all around. As one of the crew of this boat reported later, "It looked like every shark in the Bay of Bengal had homed in on her."

But there were no bodies in the water. And, since there was no acknowledgement to any signals, a boat was put out and the rescue party climbed on board.

In the chartroom they found the Captain and the ship's officers gathered as if the Captain had called them to some sort of emergency conference. They were all dead, and by now the bodies had stiffened. The decks were littered with dead crew members. The radio officer was dead in the radio room, and, down below, even the ship's dog lay dead as well.

A doctor had been put on board with the rescue party, but he could find no obvious signs of poisoning or disease, nor any way in which every living thing on board could have been suffocated. In fact, he could find no explanation at all.

The only thing they could do was take the *Ourang Medan* in tow to the nearest port and then investigate more thoroughly. And then the next astonishing thing happened.

As soon as the tow-line had been fitted, a billow of smoke began to come out of the holds, and, because without power the pumps could not be operated to put water on to the fire, the salvage crew left in a hurry, cut the tow-line and withdrew to a safe distance.

There was no reason why there should have been a fire. But then — the freighter exploded!

At the inquest and enquiry which followed, the verdict for all the people who had been on board was "death by misadventure" — because the doctor reported that something unknown had killed them. He had no alternative but to report this, of course, because there was no indication whatever of what could possibly have caused all those deaths.

Perhaps it was food poisoning, and perhaps

the ship's dog had been given the same food to eat as the men. Or perhaps it was some sort of rapidly acting disease which even the doctor could not recognize. Or the cause could have been something entirely different.

Whatever it was, there is no way now of ever discovering the truth. And, most curious of all — why had the sharks been attracted?

Chaos in the universe

The laws of science cannot be broken. To take one example, if you throw a ball into the air, it will come down to earth again. That's because of the law of gravity. It's bound to come down again unless you throw the ball, beyond the reach of gravity, into outer space. Then it will keep on going in a straight line instead.

Stars and planets move in fixed orbits. You know where they are going to be at any particular time, like the earth's movement round the sun, or the moon's orbit round the earth.

At least, everyone thought that scientific laws could not be broken until they noticed Hyperion, the moon that orbits the planet Saturn. This is a jagged object two hundred miles wide, and no one can understand its behaviour. It ought to just revolve round Saturn, but, instead, it spins in a way that cannot be predicted. Nights and days on Hyperion are absolutely random. Day or night can last any length of time.

In fact, its behaviour is complete chaos. Chaos is permanently utterly unpredictable behaviour. Even computers can't predict what's going to happen next.

But this sort of thing doesn't just happen way out in space. It also happens on earth, and the mystery is why it should, because, by all the laws of science, it is impossible.

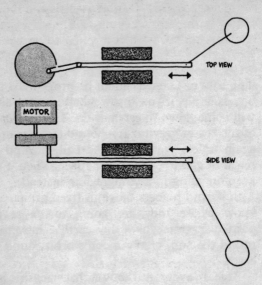

Diagram of Dr David Tritton's conical pendulum, 1987

In 1987 Dr David Tritton, of Newcastle University, devised a conical pendulum, which is one in which the suspended ball is free to move in any direction instead of just swinging from side to side. Its behaviour has astonished scientists because, when it moves, it doesn't follow any known scientific laws at all. And this reveals that the universe has an unexpected, previously unknown, and even frightening property — the ability to act in total chaos.

The conical pendulum is first made to move by electricity. While the electricity is at its normal power, the pendulum swings regularly. But, as soon as the voltage is allowed to drop, the movement of the pendulum becomes completely chaotic. It loops, whirls and swings endlessly, literally defying all known science. Nobody can tell what it is going to do next.

What's worse, even when its movements are fed into a computer, the computer can't forecast what the next movement is going to be — exactly like the movements of Hyperion.

Professor Paul Davies of Newcastle University found just part of an explanation as to why even computers can't cope with the situation. The calculations cannot keep pace with the actual movements, so all ability to predict what's going to happen next is lost. More and more computing power is needed to tell us less and less, in fact — the reverse of what *ought* to be.

It's a complete mystery. But what it can mean is that sooner or later all scientific laws *can* end up in chaos — another contradiction of what was always thought.

The pyramids of Egypt

Everyone knows why the pyramids of ancient Egypt were built, of course — they were tombs for the bodies of the Pharoahs. Each of them contains a burial chamber, with various passages either leading to it or leading round it, and in that chamber the body of the Pharoah, after it had been mummified, was placed.

Yes. That's what everyone thought for centuries. It's what most school history books still say. They were astonishing, enormous tombs, taking years to build, and they were built large enough to show the world how important Egypt and its Pharoahs were.

But there is one disturbing fact which seems to show that this was not the reason for the building of the pyramids at all. *Not a single body has ever been discovered in any of them.*

The bodies must have been stolen by grave-robbers, you might think. Well, we know that grave-robbing did take place, but what the robbers were after was the wealth of the valuables of gold, silver and precious stones inside the tombs. Usually they left the mummified bodies alone, since they weren't valuable. Also, most of those thieves operated in the Valley of the Kings, where many royal burials took place.

Let's take the Great Pyramid as an example. This was built for Pharoah Cheops, or Khufu, and is the largest pyramid of all. It was made

The Great Pyramid

with at least two and a half million blocks of
limestone, and it has an estimated weight of up
to six and a half million tons. Even now, no one
is quite sure precisely how many stone blocks
were used in its construction, nor its exact
weight.

Each side of the base of the pyramid is two
hundred and thiry yards long (210.31 metres),
and the pyramid covers an area on the ground of
13 acres (5.26 hectares). If you find difficulty in
realizing how big an area that is, or how much
stone was used in building it, Napoleon's
surveyors examined it and they estimated that,
if they removed the stone from this pyramid
and the two smaller ones not far away from it at
Giza, they could build a wall right round
France which would be three metres tall and
one metre thick. And, inside the base area, you
could place the cathedrals of Milan and

Florence, St Peter's in Rome, and Westminster Abbey, and still have room to spare!

But there's a lot more to it than that. The sides of the great pyramid of Cheops point exactly to true north, south, east and west. It is situated *exactly* between the two boundaries marking ancient Egypt, which are the lines of longitude 29°50′ east and 32°38′ east. And, if on a map, you draw a quarter-circle from the centre of the pyramid, making the lines of that arc touch those two lines of longitude, you've exactly marked out the Nile delta.

And there's a good reason why we can be sure it wasn't a tomb. In AD 820 the pyramid was opened for the first time. Caliph Abdullah Al Mamun had heard there was a secret door and passage into the pyramid which nobody had ever found, and that inside was hidden a library containing an enormous number of astronomical secrets which had since been lost. He wanted that library so he got workmen to find this secret door and passage.

There wasn't one, nor any library. But, after several attempts, the workmen at last found they had broken through, inside this huge building, to the first of many passages, which led to what is known as the King's Chamber.

There they found the sarcophagus in which the body should have been kept — but there was no lid to it. And, since this was the very first time that anyone had been inside since the pyramid was sealed, it must always have been like that. And there was no body inside!

Since the body of Pharoah Cheops could not have been removed, one possibility was that it

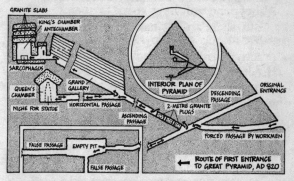

Interior plan of the Great Pyramid

had literally vanished! That, they decided, was highly unlikely, to say the least. There was only one other answer; that his body had never been placed inside the pyramid in the first place.

And the same sort of thing was discovered whenever, in later centuries, any of the pyramids were opened.

So, if the pyramids were not really tombs, just what were they for? The only likely answer is that the pyramids were placed as fixed landmarks, probably to do with astronomy and astronomical calculations. What did become clear, both then and in much later explorations of pyramids, was that they were all absolutely amazing exercises in geometry and mathematics.

But no pyramid was actually used as a tomb, no matter what school history books might still say on the matter. The whole thing is still a mystery.

Mysterious mathematics

Dr Alexander Thom, Professor of Engineering Science at Oxford University, was on a sailing holiday round the coast of Scotland. When he stepped ashore from his boat, to take a look at the ancient stone circle at Callanish, he spotted something unexpected. The circle was aligned to true north.

We have two north poles: magnetic north, to which compasses point, which moves a little from year to year, and true north, which remains in the same place all the time. Dr Thom thought that for such an ancient monument to point to true north was very odd indeed. Nowadays, you can find where north is by looking up into the sky to find the Pole Star, but, in prehistoric times, the Pole Star was in a different position from where it is now.

It could have been a coincidence that the prehistoric builders had pointed the stones in that direction, but he began to investigate. By 1967 he had checked no fewer than six hundred different ancient sites in Britain, and found that *every one* of the stone circles which he had investigated were not only lined up astronomically but were also designed in geometric patterns.

This was amazing. The problem was that prehistoric people should not have known anything at all about such mathematics. Yet, in every case, it was also found that the same unit of measurement had been used to build each of these stone circles. It is known as the "megalithic yard", or 2.72 feet. Using this, the ancient builders had constructed mathematical shapes such as ellipses, circles — and the right-angled triangle.

The use of right-angled triangles, and the correct measurements along their sides for internal constructions, should not have been known until the time of Pythagoras, a thousand years later — but all this obviously had been known. Furthermore, it was clear that the ancient, prehistoric people knew all about π. This is the mathematical relationship between the circumference (or outside edge) of a circle and its diameter (the distance across it). In every circle it is the same; if you divide the length of the circumference by the diameter, the answer is 3.142. It was first written down by Arya-Bhata in the sixth century AD. And prehistoric people should have known nothing about its existence — but they obviously did!

The most famous monument in Britain is, of course, Stonehenge. C A Hewham was able to show that, when they were standing in the centre of the great circle at Stonehenge, the ancient people were able to tell, from when the sun and moon had slipped over marker-stones on the horizon, when they had reached the limits of their orbits and a new cycle was about to begin.

The mathematics which had been used by prehistoric people was frankly astounding. As Sir Fred Hoyle, the famous British astronomer, pointed out, someone as brilliant as Newton or

Einstein "must have been at work all those thousands of years ago".

The question was, and still is, how could anyone all that long time ago have known such mathematics? Where did their knowledge come from — and why did it disappear, to be rediscovered so many centuries later?

But that isn't the end of the mystery. We know that somehow the ancient Egyptians had knowledge of this sort. It was always believed that the knowledge of the Egyptians passed slowly across Europe and was then used in ancient sites like Stonehenge. However — the

oldest monuments in Britain date from about 4500 BC on the Atlantic Ocean side, in the west, becoming gradually younger as they appear farther inland. And that's precisely the opposite direction from Egypt. The knowledge started first on the west coast of Britain, then moved gradually east, not the other way about.

So, if the knowledge didn't come from the ancient Egyptians, where did it come from?

Stonehenge

Lines of sunrise

In Britain, especially in the south of the country, ancient standing stones mark old pathways for travellers. Some of these standing stones still remain, and, if you stand at one of them, then you'll probably see another. Walk towards it in a straight line, then you'll find the next, and so on.

So these old standing stones simply marked pathways from the days before there were real roads with signposts and so on. That seemed straightforward enough until Alfred Watkins noticed something else, and in 1925 wrote his researches into a book.

What he had found was that if at sunrise on Midsummers's Day you joined up these lines, or *leys* as he called them, on a map, they also

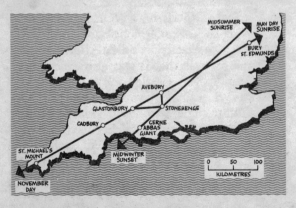

Primary Leys in southern Britain

took in the ancient ceremonial sites such as Stonehenge, the Cerne Abbas Giant (a huge prehistoric figure cut into a hill-side), and so on.

And, if you took the May Day sunrise and followed it through to exactly six months later at sunset, this produced an unbroken line on a map from Bury St Edmunds through the Avebury Circle (another ring of stones like Stonehenge and not far from it), Glastonbury, Cadbury, down to St Michael's Mount in Cornwall — all of them ancient sites. What all this this seemed to show was that all the ancient sites had not been placed just anywhere, but in a definite pattern.

Alfred Watkins wasn't the first to have noticed this sort of thing. In 1909 Sir Norman Lockyer, director of the Solar Physics Laboratory, found that, if you start at Stonehenge, the Midsummer sunrise line can be traced back exactly six miles to Grovely Castle, and, beyond there, the Cerne Abbas Giant is directly in line as well. From Stonehenge to Old Sarum, a prehistoric hill-top site where the original Salisbury Cathedral stood, was also exactly six miles. And what was even stranger was that it was also exactly six miles from Grovely Castle back to Old Sarum.

In fact, the whole layout made a perfect equilateral triangle with each side six miles long. Since then this has been known as Lockyer's Triangle. The "new" Salisbury Cathedral (built in AD 1220) was exactly in line as well, precisely two miles from Old Sarum. And beyond that, in a straight line, was Clearbury ring, another ancient site.

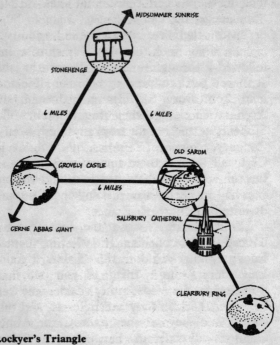

Lockyer's Triangle

Now it stands to reason that, with so many hundreds of ancient sites and pathways around, it is certain that many will line up with each other by sheer chance. Just look on a map and you're bound to be able to join up some of them. Because of this, many people took no notice of what Lockyer and Watkins had to say about them.

Just out of curiosity, though, one archaeologist tried an experiment. He knew there was evidence of a ceremonial Way from Pilsdon Pen, an early Bronze Age site on a hill in

Dorset, leading in the correct direction on May Day sunrise. So he checked on a map.

The line led directly past a standing stone, a manor house on an old site, a track to an old church — and at one end of the line was another Bronze Age site — and at the other a Norman church. But that old church had been built inside a much more ancient earthworks.

But does this actually *mean* anything? Well, it seems that it does. In France, by 1936, Xavier Guichard had discovered pretty well by chance that there was a similar alignment like the leys in Britain, only these were based on Alaise, near Besançon in southern France.

The word *Alès, Alis* or *Alles* in a place name in France originally indicated a meeting point to which people would travel. Guichard found that every place in his lines had two main features which were quite noticeable: they were all on hills which overlooked rivers, and they each had a man-made well. Also, there was the same standard distance between each of these places which make it appear that they had been placed deliberately on a particular line which can be traced along the line of the May Day sunrise. He checked four hundred such sites and found that they all fitted — right across Europe!

And, in connection with the names of places, Alfred Watkins called his lines *ley lines* because of the number of times that "ley" appeared in the names of the places through which they passed — almost exactly the same pronunciation as in the word *Alaise*. Coincidence — or what?

The entire mystery remains unsolved. And what complicates it all even further is that now evidence has been gathered from across Europe, in Britain, in Egypt and South America, and it all seems to show the same thing. Ancient sites were not chosen at random, just because people happened to be living near each of them, but in a definite plan. They were all lined up, too, in a particular way, and in planned positions.

They *seem* to be like that in connection with astronomy, either for use as observatories or at least as calendars. But why should lines of them, in addition to this, so frequently follow the path of sunrise and sunset on two days in particular in each year?

And so far there is no answer which we can discover.

Where is Atlantis?

Almost certainly the "lost land of Lyonesse" lay between Land's End, Cornwall, and the Scilly Isles, forty miles away. William of Worcester, a fifteenth century historian, quoted old monastic records which reported "a hundred and forty churches" submerged out there since the sea swept over it. Furthermore, there has always been a legend that Lyonesse was exactly in that area.

Atlantis, however, is different. It was first mentioned (and described) by Plato, the Greek philosopher, in 355 BC, who said "The fact that it is not invented fable but a genuine history is all-important." He derived his details of the lost Atlantis from Solon, who had been given the story by Egyptian priests at Sais.

Plato placed it "beyond the pillars of Hercules"— that is, beyond the Straits of Gibraltar, and so in the Atlantic Ocean. It was a great civilization, full of marvels for its day — and then it mysteriously disappeared. And it existed before the rise of the ancient Egyptians.

So then people began to look for evidence that Atlantis really had existed. It was pointed out that there are similar plants and animals on both sides of the Atlantic, so that had to be evidence that there once must have been a "land bridge" between them. That, however, is not necessarily so, as geologists now know.

There are many cross-Atlantic similarities, for example ancient monuments and pyramids, and these, people argued, must have come from one central source. That's possible, but it could be, instead, that ancient peoples were better at navigating boats than was believed. But it is true that the legend of Atlantis appears among the Greeks, the Egyptians, Celts and Europeans, and that it is equally true that the Aztecs of Mexico believed that they first arrived there from an island which they called Aztlan.

In the Atlantic is the Mid-Atlantic Ridge with the peaks of its mountains under the water still visible in various places. Proof of Atlantis? No! The ridge is actually increasing in size, and was made by purely natural causes. It has nothing to do with Atlantis.

Exactly when Atlantis existed also causes problems. The Egyptian priests told Solon that it existed in about 9600 BC, a thousand years before the rise of the ancient Egyptian civilization. But their odd method of counting was to add up the number of years in the reigns of all their kings, as shown in the king-lists. Unfortunately, on many occasions several kings had ruled at the same time in various parts of Egypt, and we now know that Egypt actually dates from about 3100 BC. So that would give the date of Atlantis as 4100 BC . . . if the Egyptians were accurate. They probably weren't!

What we know for certain is that the civilization as Plato described it was very similar indeed to the Minoan civilization which came to a sudden end in about 1500 BC. This was based on the island of Crete, in the Mediterranean, and, in about that year, there was an enormous volcanic explosion which tore the centre out of the Minoan island of Kalliste (now called Santorini) between Crete and the Greek mainland.

A tidal wave perhaps six hundred metres high resulted, sweeping away everything before it and completely destroying the Minoan empire. This was an even worse destruction than when the island of Krakatoa exploded in 1883, when three hundred towns on nearby Java and Sumatra were totally destroyed and thirty-six thousand people died. That blast was heard as far as three and a half thousand miles away at the time, in Australia, and the tidal wave even crossed the Pacific and damaged boats on the coast of South America! The volcanic dust even reached Europe.

So Plato could have got it wrong, and, in fact, Atlantis could have been not "beyond the pillars of Hercules", but actually in the Mediterranean, based on Crete.

But there is another possibility. In the first century AD, the Greek geographer, Marcellus, said that Atlantis consisted of seven islands, plus three others "of immense extent". That *could* indicate the Antilles, the West Indian islands. Or it could equally have included the continent of America, even perhaps the Mayan civilization of central America, which had a very similar system of government to that described by Plato, too.

So we have the choice — Atlantis was either part of the American continent, or the West

Indies, or the Minoan civilization. Or it did really exist *somewhere* in the Atlantic. We don't know. All we do know is that Atlantis is a likely possibility for the home of the original builders of those mysterious ancient monuments and sites which still exist in various parts of the world.

Certainly there is *something* true about the legend.

The mystery of the Dogons

Jean-Pierre Hallet, a French anthropologist, lived with the pygmies of the Ituri Forest, in central Africa, for a year and a half, studying their way of life.

What astonished him was their knowledge of the stars and planets, in particular that they called Saturn "the star of the nine moons". The fact was that Saturn's ninth moon had only been discovered by the American astronomer, W H Pickering, in 1899. Very few "civilized" people in Africa even knew that Saturn had any moons at all — and, for that matter, most Americans and Europeans didn't, either. (Did you?) What's more, the pygmies had *always* called Saturn by that name.

But the knowledge of the Ituri pygmies pales beside the totally inexplicable knowledge of the Dogons, who live south of the Sahara Desert. Even more strange, the Dogon priests inherited their knowledge from very ancient times — yet there is no way that they should have been able to do that.

The point is that the Dogons have an unbelievable knowledge of the universe. In particular, they know accurate details of a small star, absolutely invisible to the naked eye, which revolves round the star Sirius, the brightest star in the sky, and focus their attention on that.

Sirius A is the name given to the star which

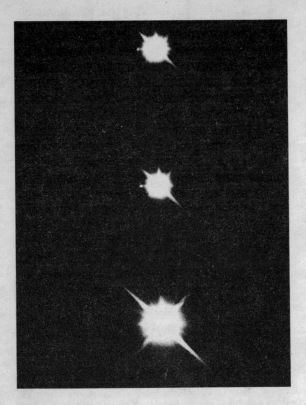

Sirius A and Sirius B

we can see, but Sirius B, the "white dwarf"
which moved round it, was not seen by anyone
until 1862, when Alvin Clark spotted it through
the most powerful telescope then invented. It is
so small, in fact, that it was not possible to
photograph it, even, until 1970. Yet the Dogons
knew all about its existence long before! Even
stranger, they know almost all there is to know
about it.

They know that it is white, that it is massively heavy (a cubic metre of it has been estimated to weigh about twenty thousand tons), that it orbits Sirius A once every fifty years, and that the orbit is elliptical and not round. In addition, they know all about the halo which surrounds Saturn — and that is completely impossible to detect with the human eye — about the four main moons of the planet Jupiter, that the planets revolve round the sun, that the earth is more or less round in shape and spins on its own axis, and that the Milky Way is spiral-shaped. (And that last fact wasn't known by astronomers until fairly recently.)

The next point is that they could not possibly have been told such detailed information by any explorers. Explorers are not normally experts in astronomy! But what is even more astonishing is how the Dogons themselves explain where their knowledge comes from.

Visitors from a planet attached to Sirius B landed on earth and passed the information on to them, they say! More, they call the creatures who landed Nommos, and say they were amphibians. They arrived in an "ark" which came down spinning or whirling, and landed in a whirlwind of dust.

Now that might sound ridiculous, except that the historian, Robert Temple, was able to trace that the Dogons are the last people on earth to worship extra-terrestrial amphibians who were supposed to have landed in the Persian Gulf before civilization began anywhere, and which appear in the drawings and legends of the gods of ancient Babylon, Egypt and Greece.

There is certainly a close resemblance between Nommo and the amphibian god of ancient Babylon, known as Oannes. Oannes was said to have been some kind of superior being who, with his companions, taught the people of ancient Sumer how to write, plus mathematics, astronomy and agriculture.

According to all that remains of a history of Babylon written in Greek by a priest named Borossus, Oannes was described as having a body like that of a fish "and it had under a fish's head another head, and also feet below, similar to those of a man, joined to the fish's tail". He had a human voice, and at sunset each day would go into the sea, "for he was amphibious".

Maybe not so much a fish as some kind of creature in a space suit? But, if so, why go into the water each night?

There is something very mysterious about all this. No one knew of the Dogon knowledge until Marcel Griaule and Germaine Dieterlen discovered it by living with them from 1946 until 1950 when it was revealed to them. It has since been discovered that they were not making it all up, either! When Griaule died in 1956, two hundred and fifty thousand Africans appeared at his funeral in Mali, in tribute.

In ancient Babylon, the chief "fish-man" was called Oannes or Oe. In Sumer, north-east from there, he was called Enki or Ea. The Philistines worshipped two amphibious gods, Dagon and Atargatis — and Atargatis was the "Syrian goddess" who came to earth from an "egg". The Telchines, who appeared on the Greek island of Rhodes and were described as civilizers, were according to legends "submarine magic spirits" and "demons of the depths of the sea".

Strange, isn't it? Visitors from outer space, some of them having to live in water for part of the time? It doesn't seem entirely credible!

But, if it isn't, where did the Dogon tribes obtain their ancient knowledge from? They say that they know . . .

Who was Fyodor Kuzmitch?

On 23rd March, 1801, Tsar Paul I of Russia was murdered in an uprising in the palace, and his son, Alexander, became the new Tsar at the age of twenty-three. Whereas Paul had been feared and hated, Alexander ended all torture, tried to improve the government, and tried to make peace with Napoleon.

Napoleon's French Army, though, invaded Russia in 1812. But a severe winter came early and they had to retreat. Many died, and, of the rest, half were taken prisoner by the Russians. Alexander's prestige rose even higher as a result, especially when, soon afterwards, he called together all the rulers of Europe and persuaded them to sign that they would never go to war again.

The trouble was that none of Alexander's ideas and reforms ever really worked, no matter how hard he tried. He became depressed about this and, in 1819, named his younger brother, Nicholas, as his successor. "Europe needs strong, young, monarchs," he said. "I think it is my duty to retire in time."

Nobody believed that he meant this, because Tsars never retired — they remained the rulers of Russia until they died. But then, in 1825, something strange happened. First Alexander's wife, the Empress, became ill. He took her to Tagonrog, a small town a thousand miles from the capital, St Petersburg (now called

Tsar Alexander I of Russia

Leningrad), and rented a villa.

In October he decided to inspect the Russian troops in the Crimea, and, when he came back in the middle of November, had a chill and a high temperature. On 1st December, 1825, he died.

Or did he? In 1919 his coffin was found to be empty. In addition, there's something odd about the medical reports of 1825, and here's where the mystery begins. Whereas Prince Volkonsky wrote that he spent a good night, his English doctor, Sir James Wylie, reported that he was getting worse. When Wylie noted that Alexander was feverish, a letter from the Empress said that he was feeling well. And, when both Prince Volkonsky and the Empress at the same time noted that his condition was unchanged, Sir James Wylie noted instead that he was much better.

And, although Tsar Alexander was very religious, no priest was ever called. Furthermore, when the post-mortem, or autopsy, was carried out on the body, not only did the body not seem to be Alexander's, but one of the doctors, Dr Dimitri Tarassov, who was supposed to have signed the death certificate, said his signature was a forgery.

What's more, all pages of the Empress's diary after 23rd November, plus a personal letter which Alexander wrote to his mother, vanished completely. But one letter, written to his brother Constantine, did survive. In it Alexander said that he'd let him know when he was going to abdicate, and then Constantine could tell their mother.

Ten years later, the mystery deepened. In 1836, a stranger rode on a white horse into a Siberian village to have his horse shod. He refused to tell the local police who he was, was arrested and sentenced to flogging and imprisonment. Grand Duke Michael, Alexander's youngest brother, promptly appeared in the village and threatened severe punishment if they did any such thing to the stranger. He also had a long talk with the prisoner, who was then released.

Then, in 1842, the same stranger became a hermit in a hut in a forest at Krasnorechensk, calling himself Fyodor Kuzmitch. He was a very strange sort of hermit, however. He wrote letters regularly to many Russian notables, including the future Tsar Alexander II, who seemed to know him well. And, on one occasion, a retired soldier suddenly came across him and said, "It's the Tsar!"

Fyodor replied that he was just a vagabond, and, if the soldier went round saying things like that, the soldier would be put into prison and the hermit would be forced to move on.

He saw to the education of a clever peasant girl and, in 1849, sent her off to visit the holy places of central Russia. He gave her letters of introduction to many Russian nobles, including Count Dimitri Osten-Sacken, who as a result invited her to stay with him. While she was there, she saw a full-length portrait of Tsar Alexander I and announced that he looked exactly like Fyodor Kuzmitch, even to the way they both stood with both hands on their belts!

In 1859, the girl left to marry an Army major and lived in Kiev until her husband died in 1864. Then she went back to see the hermit again. In the meantime he'd died, too, but she did discover something more about him.

When Fyodor had died, what they had found on him was a small pouch which he wore on a cord round his neck. In it was a coded message from Tsar Paul to his wife: "We have discovered a terrible flaw in our son. Count Pahlen informs me of Alexander's part in the conspiracy. We must hide tonight, wherever it is possible."

So was Fyodor Kuzmitch really Tsar Alexander I of Russia? And if not — who could he have been? And, if he was really the Tsar, did he become a hermit because of the shame of having been part of the conspiracy which resulted in the murder of his father?

What happened to the Dauphin?

The eldest son of a King of France was known as the Dauphin. After the French Revolution, when King Louis XVI and Queen Marie-Antoinette had been guillotined, the only members of the French royal family left alive were the Dauphin, Louis-Charles, and his sister, Marie-Thérèse.

Marie-Thérèse and Louis-Charles as children

Both children were allowed to stay with their mother in prison in the Temple, Paris, until the night of 3rd July, 1793. During that night, six officers came in and dragged him away. He was eight years old at the time.

He was made to live with a cobbler, Antoine Simon, until January, 1794. Then he was taken back to a small, dark room at the top of the Temple. The room had no windows, only an iron grille over the door. Food and bedclothes were passed to him through this. Then they stopped supplying him with bedclothes. There was no lavatory, and the guards kept themselves at a distance because of the stench. The food was poor, and he was not allowed anything to drink.

Then it was announced that Louis-Charles, aged ten years and two months, had died on 8th June, 1795, from tuberculosis. However, nobody in his family had ever suffered from that, and he couldn't have caught it. In addition, the doctors who were called in were required only to *examine* the corpse and decide on the *probable* cause of death, not to identify it!

Rumours began that he had been poisoned, starved or beaten to death. In May, a Dr Desault had been called in to treat the boy. He died suddenly and mysteriously soon afterwards, and his widow said it was because he had refused to take part in some "irregular practice" in the boy's cell. She also said that the Dauphin had not died, but had been rescued and another boy put in to take his place.

In 1846 the coffin was opened and the skeleton examined. Even stranger now — the body was about the right size, but the arms and legs were far too big, as if belonging to a much older boy. And the skull contained a wisdom tooth — and they don't appear until about the age of eighteen or so, not at the age of ten.

So what did happen to the Dauphin? Did he really survive, or didn't he? Of the forty or so who later claimed to be him, just two people need noting.

John James Audubon was a very famous artist in North America, specializing in paintings of birds. He was supposed to have been the illegitimate son of a French naval officer, but he had no birth certificate when he was adopted by Mr Audubon on 7th March, 1794 — two months after the cobbler, Antoine Simon, stopped looking after the prince. And, after Simon gave him up, hardly anyone but guards ever saw the prince, it might be noted.

On a visit to Paris in 1828, Audubon wrote to his wife in Kentucky that there he was in Paris, and that "I, who should command all", instead "dressed as a common man walk the streets". He certainly seemed to know more of his true background than he was prepared to tell most people!

In France, in 1834, a man calling himself Comte de Richemont, but actually a con-man who had used at least a dozen different names, was put on trial for claiming to be Prince Louis-Charles, the lost Dauphin. He would have been of no real interest except for what happened during the trial, since many people were prepared to believe him and he was becoming famous.

A mysterious "man in black" suddenly entered the court and handed to the judge an enormous document sealed with the arms of France. He had come to protest about the claims of this imposter, he said, on behalf of the real Dauphin, a German clock-maker calling himself Karl Wilhelm Nouendorff! That sounded ludicrous, until the claim was investigated.

Nouendorff *looked* like a member of the Bourbon family. When he was questioned by Louis-Charles's childhood nurse, he could answer all her questions about little childhood incidents, and when she tried to trick him by showing him a blue coat which she had kept, and said he had worn it in Paris on a special occasion, he pointed out that he'd only worn that coat at Versailles. She was convinced.

The Dauphin's sister, now the Duchesse d'Angoulême, refused to meet him. Instead, the French government deported him. He settled in the Netherlands, and died at Delft in 1845. On his tombstone it declared he was the rightful King of France.

Whilst what the tombstone said proved nothing, something even stranger happened. In 1863 the Dutch government authorized his son to use the name "de Bourbon". And, when in November, 1913, a journalist disputed the family's right to the Bourbon name, a *French* court not only upheld that right but fined the journalist for libel! There is certainly something odd somewhere!

So — if the Dauphin didn't die of his ill-treatment, was he later known as Audubon, the famous artist, in America, or was he instead Karl Wilhelm Nouendorff, the German clock-maker? In both cases, the supposed dates of birth fitted almost exactly.

One thing is certain — Louis-Charles couldn't have been both of them.

People who vanish

Supposing somebody is running along the road in front of you, stumbles, then *vanishes* in mid-air before his body reaches the ground, while you watch! You wouldn't believe it unless you actually saw it, would you? Yet precisely this has actually happened.

On 3rd September, 1873, James Worson, a shoemaker of Leamington Spa, Warwickshire, bet he could run from Leamington Spa to Coventry in record time. Two friends followed in a horse-drawn, two-wheeled carriage, and they had a camera with them.

After Worson had run about five miles, he suddenly stumbled as if he had tripped over an uneven patch of ground, fell forward, screamed — and vanished in mid-air. All that was left of him were his footprints in the soft ground, ending as suddenly as if he had run into an invisible wall, and they were photographed.

The police and volunteers searched the whole area between Leamington Spa and Coventry. All they ever found were James Worson's last footprints on the unmade road, and that was where the bloodhounds lost all scent of him, too.

He is not the only one to whom this has happened, either. In 1809, Benjamin Bathurst of the British Foreign Office was in Berlin. He told his valet to stand by the carriage door while he inspected the horses, walked to where the horses stood — and was never seen again.

On 23rd September, 1880, David Lang of Gallatin, Tennessee, USA, was walking across a field towards his wife, children and two visitors who had arrived at his farm. The visitors were Judge Pack and the Judge's brother-in-law. David Lang took perhaps a dozen steps towards them, in full view of them all, then quite simply he was he longer there. He had disappeared completely!

The Judge, seeing there was no possible hole into which Lang could have fallen, organized a search party with the help of the neighbours, and they even searched the nearby woods and continued at night using lanterns.

The county surveyor was sent for, to find if there were any caves or potholes into which he could have fallen. There was none. There was no possible way in which David Lang could have fallen underground. The search continued, totally unsuccessfully, for many months.

But, where he had vanished, a circle of withered grass eventually appeared, the only withered grass anywhere on the farm.

These are just three of the cases where a person has inexplicably vanished while others watched. Others have vanished, but not while they were being observed. But one person *almost* vanished.

The American magician, William Neff, was performing during an afternoon performance at the Paramount Theatre, New York. Very slowly he began to fade during the performance until finally the stage curtains behind him could be seen through him. Then he slowly became solid again, apparently not realizing what had happened.

Everyone thought it was part of the show, and was done by trickery, until it was revealed that this had happened only twice before — once on stage in Chicago, and once at home in front of his wife who was terrified at what she saw happening!

Time slips

Arthur and Mary Guirdham, who lived in Bath, Somerset, were on holiday in Yorkshire. One day they drove to a town fifteen miles from where they were staying. In the evening they began to drive back again, but, since it was a warm and pleasant evening, they decided to take their time over it.

After about five minutes, they suddenly came across a signpost which they didn't believe because it said they were now only three miles from where they were staying. So they stopped to look at a map. The signpost was right. They were only three miles from their hotel, as they discovered as they drove on.

That meant they had driven twelve miles in five minutes . . . a speed of about a hundred and forty-two miles an hour!

This was quite impossible. First, they had been driving slowly, and secondly, had they kept up an average speed of over a hundred miles an hour, somebody would certainly have noticed. So what had happened to them during that mysterious five minutes?

The plain answer is that nobody knows. It was one of those instances, fortunately rare, where either time or distance seems to have telescoped. It has happened before, when people appear to have moved virtually simultaneously from one place to another. Even if we discount tales from people who have claimed to have been captured by aliens from a UFO — which no one can prove and which usually happens in very suspicious circumstances anyway — some very strange things are known to have happened.

Take the case of Sister Mary of the convent at Agredo, in Spain. Between 1620 and 1631 she repeatedly claimed that she kept being transported to Mexico to convert the Jumano Indians. She was regarded as either hysterical — or mad. But then there was a complaint.

Father Alonzo de Benavides had been given the job of converting the Mexican Indians, but he wrote to both the Pope and to King Philip IV of Spain that somebody else was there — a mysterious nun kept appearing, whom the Indians called the "lady in blue", who gave out crosses and rosaries, and had a chalice with which the Indians celebrated Mass. He wanted to know who she was.

Nobody knew, but when Father de Benavides returned to Spain in 1630 he heard of Sister Mary and went to investigate. She was able to give details of Mexican Indian customs and of the villages where the Indians lived. At that time, very few Europeans had ever travelled there, so she couldn't have learned these from travellers. She had never left the convent, according to her superiors, and what was more, it turned out that the chalice which the Indians had used had actually come from that convent.

Even more, her presence was recorded by Spanish soldiers, French explorers, and even by different tribes of Indians living thousands of miles apart, all of whom had seen her. Altogether, she seemed to have been transported — if that's the right word — about five hundred times from Spain to Mexico.

In 1906, three children disappeared. The difference is, these children had no idea of what had happened to them. In Gloucester, the children of the Vaughan family, a ten-year-old boy and his two sisters, aged eight and seven, went into a field near their home and vanished.

For three days a search was made for them, but, on the fourth day, they were all found asleep in a ditch at the edge of the same field from which they had vanished, a place which had already been searched several times before.

They were not hungry, and they had no idea that they had been missing for three days. And, even years later, when they were all grown up, they still could recall nothing at all of what had happened to them or offer any explanation.

In 1928 the Marquis Carlo Scotto vanished from a locked room, only to turn up in a nearby stable — which was also locked. Again, there was no sensible explanation, and the Marquis himself couldn't explain it, either.

There is no doubt, however, that all of this happened — but how it happened remains a complete mystery.

The devil's footprints

There has never been an explanation for what happened on the night of 8th February, 1855. Snow covered most of the ground in the county of Devon, and, when people woke in the morning, they found an unbroken line of footprints stretching from Totnes to Exmouth.

And it really was an unbroken line. The mysterious footprints ran in a straight line across farms and gardens, along streets, down lanes, and, where there was an obstacle such as a building, over the roof! At a fourteen-foot high wall they stopped at one side to re-appear on the other. Where a river was crossed, the marks led to the bank of the river, then carried on at the far side. And they stretched for a distance of about fifteen miles.

Because it was a severe winter, the marks remained in the snow for days, and hundreds of people saw them. They were something like the marks left by a donkey, but they were a *single* line of footprints, as if made by a *two-legged* donkey marching carefully with one foot always exactly in front of the other.

Various suggestions were made at the time, varying from an unknown animal which had escaped from a zoo, to an unknown monster which had come ashore from the sea — and the devil!

What we know for certain is that the snow that night was about three-quarters of an inch

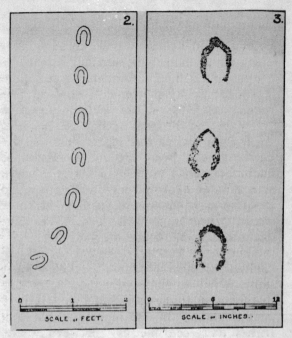

The devil's footprints

deep (about 19 millimetres), showing also
marks left by dogs, cats, rabbits and birds. The
marks appeared on a window-sill at Marley
House near Exmouth, two storeys up from the
ground. And, in the middle of a field near
Exmouth, the only gap in the line appeared —
the marks appeared in the middle of the field, all
pointing in the same direction but "without any
apparent approach or retreat" according to the
local vicar, the Reverend Ellecombe.

Also, at one point, the tracks spread wider
and doubled, then turned into a single track as

before.

When it happened again, it was still in Devon, only this time it was in February, 1963. This time the marks were seen and sketched by two people who lived at Mannamead, and, quite independently, by another in Noss Mayo. The woman at Noss Mayo actually heard a "terrifying howl" from outside her house at about eight o'clock that night while she was having a bath. Being a country-woman, she knew the sounds made by different animals, such as foxes, but could not identify this sound at all — except it was so horrible she never wanted to hear anything like it again! Then, the next morning, she found the footprints.

They were exactly the same as on the previous occasion, a hundred and eight years previously. The marks were four inches long and two and a quarter inches wide (about 10 centimetres by 5.7 centimetres), with eight inches (20 centimetres) between them, sometimes just a little more.

There is one interesting point — the footprints were visible because there was snow on the ground. Suppose there had been no snow. The marks would not then have appeared. But would that mean that the creature would still have actually been there, but leaving no marks behind it?

In fact, does some sort of devil — if that was what really caused the footprints — walk about regularly, and we don't know about it? And, if so, what is it?

The Yeti

What strange creature can possibly live high up in the Himalayas? It's known as the Yeti, or "Abominable Snowman", and perhaps the first report of its existence by a European came from B H Hodson. He was an English explorer who, in 1832, had been in Nepal, and he said it was a tall, ape-like creature which was covered in thick hair and was living high up in the mountains.

Everyone thought he must have seen either a Himalayan red bear or a Langur monkey. Langur monkeys have been seen at altitudes above four thousand metres. They sometimes stand upright on two legs for a while, and are quite large.

But then, in 1887, Major Waddell, of the Indian Army Medical Corps, reported finding huge footprints in the snow at Sikkim which didn't belong to either of these two creatures, but which he couldn't otherwise identify.

Then, in November, 1921, William Knight said he had definitely seen a Yeti. The chances are, though, that he was mistaken. Almost certainly he had come across a *sadhu*, or Hindu hermit, who live at altitudes of about five thousand metres, and so was a real human being.

However, in the same year, Colonel Howard-Bury was leading an expedition up Mount Everest when he and his party all saw a group of strange creatures at about five thousand one hundred metres, and, when they went to investigate, discovered footprints which were about three times larger than those of a human being, though the creatures who had made them had gone.

His sherpas told him they were Yeti tracks, but he couldn't bring himself to believe that he'd actually seen the Yeti and decided they must be wolf tracks instead. But, of course, the size of the footprints was wrong. There was no doubt now that there was *something* high up in the mountains, but the question was — what?

Within four years some sort of answer was found. Major-General Topilsky of the Russian army was with his troops in the Pamir Mountains of southern Russia, searching for rebels, in 1925. They found some prints of large bare feet heading towards a cliff face. Then a noise was heard coming from a cave. The troops fired, expecting the sound to be caused by rebels, but instead out came a hairy ape-man!

He was covered in hair apart from his knees, feet, face and hands. He had a slanting forehead, a protruding jaw-bone and a flat nose. That they discovered as he fell dead. Because they were unable to take the body with them, the troops buried it underneath some stones and left. The creature looked exactly like pictures of Neanderthal man.

We still have no photographs, however — or at least, none of the Yeti itself. But what we do have are some remarkable photographs taken by Eric Shipton in November, 1951. He, with Michael Ward and Sherpa Tensing, were at about six and a half thousand metres up Mount Everest when they came across a line of footprints in the snow. Shipton photographed them.

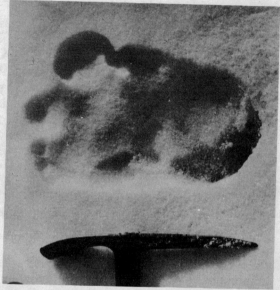

Shipton's photograph of a Yeti footprint, 1951

Now, suppose that some creature such as a mountain goat had walked through the snow, then the snow had melted, making the footprints expand, and then the snow had frozen again. The result would be enormous footprints, wouldn't it?

However, one of the photographs defies any such explanation. The footprint which it shows is human in shape, but about thirteen inches long and eight inches wide (33 centimetres long and 20 centimetres wide). Even the separate toes are clearly visible. This was made by no mountain goat — and if it was caused by a humanoid type of creature, it would have to be about eight feet (2.43 metres) tall!

In the 1960s, Dr Jeanne Kofman set up a base in the Caucasus to study the Almas or "wild men" who were reputed to live in Mongolia. She reported her findings in Moscow in 1966. She had interviewed three hundred people, and rejected about a hundred of their accounts as not being reliable enough. On the other hand, two lairs were found in which the creatures had obviously been living, and nearly thirty witnesses has seen an Alma girl searching for corn-cobs nearby. She had left footprints — and teeth-marks in cobs which she had thrown away.

So, is the Yeti — and the Alma — some kind of descendant of Neanderthal man. — those early humans who *should* have died out thousands of years ago? It is very possible. We shan't know for certain until a *clear* photograph is produced of an actual creature, or a body.

Because, there is another mystery — where do the bodies go when the creatures die? The only body ever recovered was that of the one which was shot in 1925, and that has never been found again, not even its skeleton.

Bigfoot and Sasquatch

In the mountains and forests which stretch in a wilderness from California in America to British Columbia in Canada lurk ape-like creatures of no known species. In America, the creature is known as Bigfoot, and, in Canada, the Sasquatch. There is no doubt of its existence.

In the nineteenth century, an explorer named David Thomas became the first European to find signs of its existence — a footprint fourteen inches (35.36 centimetres) long. Two of the creatures attacked a prospector at Mount St Helen's, Washington in 1918. In 1924, a lumberman, camping opposite Vancouver Island, was actually kidnapped by one of them! After a week he escaped and said that the Sasquatch family consisted of an eight-foot male, a six-foot female and two children.

In the same year, there was a battle between prospectors and a group of the creatures at a place called Ape Canyon, in Oregon, after a prospector had shot one of them. A great deal of damage resulted.

In 1940, at Ruby Creek, British Columbia, Mrs Chapman and her daughter ran from their farmhouse when they found a Sasquatch coming menacingly towards it. It was about eight feet tall, or two and a half metres, they said. It overturned a barrel of salted fish, followed them to the river, had a drink, and then seemed to lose interest.

They are known to eat berries. One was seen in 1955, from a short distance away, putting branches into its mouth and stripping off the leaves. In 1967, three of them were seen at a nest of rats, "eating them like bananas". And it seems that they like chocolate. In 1958, on a construction site where the Bluff Creek road was being built, in northern California, a construction worker was woken by a noise, opened the door of his shack and found an enormous hairy creature standing outside. He gave it a bar of chocolate and it ran off with it!

They are enormously strong. We know that because, on the same construction site, one night a fifty-gallon drum of oil was carried by one across the site. The men chased it in a lorry, but it ran off.

In 1967, Roger Patterson was tracking through the forests near Bluff Creek when he saw a female Bigfoot not far away. He had a movie camera with him, and photographed the creature with it.

But, very strangely, as with the Yeti, no bones or bodies have ever been found. Incredibly, because of this fact, it is still suggested that Bigfoot and Sasquatch don't actually exist, and that people are making up all the stories about them. However, there is no doubt of their existence. One was captured as long ago as 1884, and there is no doubt about that.

A driver of a train in Fraser River Valley, British Columbia, saw a hairy creature asleep

Patterson's photograph of a Bigfoot, 1967

beside the track. So, he stopped the train, the crew gave chase and captured it by knocking it unconscious with a rock. They named it Jacko and took it with them to Yale, the next town along the line.

It was described in the newspaper, the *Victoria Colonist*, as human in form but covered all over with inch-long hair except for its hands and feet. It was young, only four feet seven inches tall (about 140 centimetres), and weighed a hundred and twenty-seven pounds (57.6 kilograms). It ate berries and drank milk. Unfortunately it died while being crated up for another train journey — as an exhibit in a travelling side-show! And nobody had the sense to take a photograph!

And still nobody knows to what species Bigfoot and the Sasquatch belong. It's some sort of ape — we know that. But there shouldn't be any apes in that part of the world. So its origin is a complete mystery.

The Province of Carolana

No one knows for certain what happened. In fact, not until late in 1987 did anyone know that anything had happened at all. But then Dr Kenneth Brown of the University of Houston, Texas, excavated a site at Houston and found the remains of a settlement on land near Buffalo Bayou, now the Houston Ship Canal.

King Charles I granted a charter to Sir Robert Heath to develop all the land in America that lay between latitude 30 and latitude 36, except for any lands already owned by a Christian king. That area stretches from the Atlantic to the Pacific, from as far south as what is now Houston and New Orleans to as far north as Oklahoma City. So what happened?

We know what Sir Robert intended to do, because he planned plantations, the sending out of settlers, and so on, and this enormous territory was going to be called Carolana. Until 1987, however, it was thought that nothing more was done about it.

The Spanish established the first European settlement in that part of the world at Ysleta, about ten miles from El Paso, in 1681 or 1682. The French moved in and also attempted to colonize what later became Texas, and the first British settlers did not appear until the early 1800s.

At least, that was what was always thought until Dr Brown began his excavation. It would have been a good, safe place for a plantation, he decided, and it must have been a large colony which had lived there all those years ago. What he found particularly were some bones, some salt-glaze pottery — and lines of graves for more than sixty bodies. There was also evidence that a small church had been built. And it was an English colony, not a Spanish or French one.

The pottery dated from the time of Charles I, and, curiously, the graves were black-earth English graves of an unusual kind. The colonists seemed to have buried their dead in accordance with a law passed in England in 1563, when it was believed that plague or smallpox victims could infect anyone who came into contact even with the earth over their dead bodies.

So, it seems that the establishment of the Province of Carolana did actually begin, with this large settlement, but that then disaster overtook it, probably some kind of epidemic which wiped it out.

The mystery is how such a large settlement arrived in America without any apparent records of its existence, and why, when it disappeared, no one seemed to know or even enquire. By the time the Spaniards arrived at Ysleta, the English colonists must already have been burying their dead, their existence unknown to anyone else.

The Australian UFO

Unidentified Flying Objects — UFOs — are not exactly something new. In 1816, for example, a great many people living in Edinburgh were astonished and scared to see a large, luminous, crescent-shaped object flying over the city, with no idea of what it could possibly be.

In 1879, a British warship in the Persian Gulf reported that two huge "spinning aerial discs" had been seen just above sea level. In November, 1883, a pulsating, disc-like object passed over the city of Santiago, South America. And in November, 1887, a large green mottled disc was observed in the sky from the Greenwich Observatory, London, and the same disc was also reported from elsewhere in Europe.

In this century, UFO sightings have taken place in France, Belgium, Italy, Brazil, Australia, Canada and the United States . . . and elsewhere, mainly dating from about 1954 onwards.

But there are two problems. The first is that objects which have been mistaken for UFOs have included fireflies, space satellites, light reflections in car windows and windscreens, the planet Venus, and weather balloons! The other problem is that, very often, hard evidence is completely lacking. One person, or maybe two, have *claimed* to have seen a UFO, while nobody else in the vicinity has seen anything of the sort.

However, there are exceptions, and one of the strangest events took place on 19th January, 1988. This happened on a road near Mundrabilla, on the Eyre road in the South Australian desert.

A woman and her three sons were in a car. The woman was Fay Knowles, aged forty-eight, and her sons were Patrick, aged twenty-four, Sean, aged twenty-one, and Wayne, aged eighteen. They found themselves being followed along the desert road by a "huge, bright, glowing object". As if that wasn't enough, the car, they said, was suddenly sucked up into the air by it!

When they reported the curious affair to the police at the coastal town of Ceduna, three hundred and seventy miles away, Police Sergeant James Fennel was naturally disbelieving. But, when he inspected the car, he found it covered in a thick coating of black ash, which had also got inside the car and there was damage to the car's roof. The tyre of one of the rear wheels had also blown and the spare wheel had had to be used.

What the family of four reported was that the "object" flew over the car and suddenly sucked it into the air and then dropped it back on to the road, blowing out the rear tyre. Something else happened, they said. Their voices had become slurred at the time of the incident, and they could only speak very slowly.

Even with four people in a car, however, it was still possible that they had concocted the story between them. Perhaps black ash had fallen on the car from somewhere. Perhaps then they had had a burst tyre, put the two together and then invented the rest.

But then other reports began to come in. The same glowing object had been seen by other people as well, hundreds of miles apart from each other, so there was no way in which they could all have conspired to invent a story.

A truck driver complained to the police that his truck had been followed on the road by something flying along behind him in the sky and glowing. A Tuna Spotter aircraft reported that an unexplained bright light had been seen near the road on which the Knowles family had been travelling. And then, shortly afterwards, the crew of a fishing trawler out at sea in the Australian Bight reported seeing what appeared to be the same object hovering not far away from them.

There is no explanation. Even if we disregard all the sightings of objects which can be explained, or which are doubtful because so few people claim to have seen the happening, just under two per cent have no logical explanation at all.

And the Australian unexplained flying object is perhaps the most mystifying of them all so far.

ACKNOWLEDGEMENTS

The photographs in this book are reproduced with the permission of:
The Fortean Picture Library 7, 27, 83, 91; The Illustrated London News Picture Library 10; BBC Hulton Picture Library 16, 45, 50, 67, 71; Keystone Press Agency 20; Northern Lighthouse Board 30; Royal Geographical Society 87; the Lick Observatory, California 62.

Diagrams by David Farris

HIPPO NON-FICTION BOOKS

Hippo Books have got all sorts of fascinating non-fiction books to suit a whole variety of interests. Whether you're interested in sport, animals or pop stars, there's something for everyone to enjoy!

The Olympic Fun Book   £2.95
You'll find fun facts about past Olympic games, amazing stories, a Go for Gold quiz, photographs, puzzles and loads of information in this book that's a must for all those interested in the most important sports event of 1988.

Wimbledon Tennis Stars   £2.95
Facts, figures and lots of fabulous photographs of all the top tennis players. Find out more about your favourite tennis stars — just in time for Wimbledon!

A-Ha   £2.50
Fabulous photographs, inside stories and stacks of information about one of the most successful young bands around today.

Working Animals: Danny the Guide Dog   £1.95
**   Lloyd the Police Horse   £1.95**
**   Mist the Sheepdog   £1.95**

If you're interested in animals you'll enjoy this series which looks at animals who work for people. They contain beautiful colour photographs and all sorts of information about working animals.

HIPPO BOOKS FOR OLDER READERS

If you enjoy a good read, look out for all the Hippo books that are available for older readers. You'll find gripping adventure stories, romance novels, spooky ghost stories and all sorts of fun fiction.

CHEERLEADERS 2: GETTING EVEN	Christopher Pike	£1.25
CHEERLEADERS 3: RUMOURS	Caroline B Cooney	£1.25
ANIMAL INN 1: PETS ARE FOR KEEPS	Virginia Vail	£1.50
MEGASTAR	Jean Ure	£1.50
SOMERSAULTS	Michael Hardcastle	£1.50
THE LITTLE GYMNAST	Sheila Haigh	£1.25
CREEPS	Tim Schoch	£1.50
THE GREAT FLOOD MYSTERY	Jane Curry	£1.75
GET LAVINIA GOODBODY!	Roger Collinson	£1.25
AM I GOING WITH YOU?	Thurley Fowler	£1.25
THE KARATE KID: PART II	B. B. Hiller	£1.25
KEVIN AND THE IRON POODLE	J. K. Hooper	£1.25

You'll find these and many more fun Hippo books at your local bookseller, or you can order them direct. Just send off to *Customer Services, Hippo Books, Westfield Road, Southam, Leamington Spa, Warwickshire CV33 0JH*, not forgetting to enclose a cheque or postal order for the price of the book(s) plus 30p per book for postage and packing.

HIPPO CLASSICS

If you have enjoyed this book why not move on to some of the following books from the Hippo Classic list. Each one a great read — and such good value!

LITTLE WOMEN	Louisa M Alcott	£1.00
THE HOUND OF THE BASKERVILLES	Sir Arthur Conan Doyle	£1.00
THE WIND IN THE WILLOWS	Kenneth Grahame	£1.00
THE RAILWAY CHILDREN	E Nesbit	£1.00
HEIDI	Johanna Spyri	£1.00
TREASURE ISLAND	Robert L Stevenson	£1.00
THE ADVENTURES OF TOM SAWYER	Mark Twain	£1.00
AROUND THE WORLD IN EIGHTY DAYS	Jules Verne	£1.00

You'll find these and many more fun Hippo books at your local bookseller, or you can order them direct. Just send off to *Customer Services, Hippo Books, Westfield Road, Southam, Leamington Spa, Warwickshire CV33 0JH*, not forgetting to enclose a cheque or postal order for the price of the book(s) plus 30p per book for postage and packing.

HIPPO BESTSELLERS

If you enjoyed this book, why not look out for other bestselling Hippo titles. You'll find gripping novels, fun activity books, fascinating non-fiction, crazy humour and sensational poetry books for all ages and tastes.

THE GHOSTBUSTERS STORYBOOK	Anne Digby	£2.50
SNOOKERED	Michael Hardcastle	£1.50
BENJI THE HUNTED	Walt Disney Company	£2.25
NELLIE AND THE DRAGON	Elizabeth Lindsay	£1.75
ALIENS IN THE FAMILY	Margaret Mahy	£1.50
HARRIET AND THE CROCODILES	Martin Waddell	£1.25
MAKE ME A STAR 1: PRIME TIME	Susan Beth Pfeffer	£1.50
THE SPRING BOOK	Troy Alexander	£2.25
SLEUTH	Sherlock Ransford	£1.50
THE SPOOKTACULAR JOKE BOOK	Theodore Freek	£1.25
ROLAND RAT'S RODENT JOKE BOOK		£1.25
THE LITTLE VAMPIRE	Angela Sommer-Bodenberg	£1.25
POSTMAN PAT AND THE GREENDALE GHOST	John Cunliffe	£1.50
POSTMAN PAT AND THE CHRISTMAS PUDDING	John Cunliffe	£1.50

You'll find these and many more fun Hippo books at your local bookseller, or you can order them direct. Just send off to *Customer Services, Hippo Books, Westfield Road, Southam, Leamington Spa, Warwickshire CV33 0JH*, not forgetting to enclose a cheque or postal order for the price of the book(s) plus 30p per book for postage and packing.

HIPPO ACTIVITY BOOKS

Feeling bored? Get into some of these activity books on the Hippo list — from Postman Pat to Defenders of the Earth, there is plenty of fun to be had by all!

THE DISNEY QUIZ AND PUZZLE BOOK	The Walt Disney Company	£0.99
THE DISNEY QUIZ AND PUZZLE BOOK IV	The Walt Disney Company	£1.25
MILES OF FUN	Penny Kitchenham	£1.95
ADVENTURE IN SPACE	Janet McKellar and Jenny Bullough	£1.95
THE HAUNTED CASTLE		
THE COUNTRYSIDE ACTIVITY BOOK		
THE DINOSAUR FUN BOOK	Gillian Osband	£1.95
THE ANTI-COLOURING BOOK	Susan Striker	£2.75
THE MAGIC MIRROR BOOK	Marion Walter	£1.75
THE SECOND MAGIC MIRROR BOOK	Marion Walter	£1.50
THE INTERPLANETARY TOY BOOK	J Alan Williams	£2.25
THE SUMMER ACTIVITY BOOK	Hannah Glease	£2.25
THE HOLIDAY FUN BOOK		£1.95
POSTMAN PAT'S SONGBOOK	Bryan Daly	£1.75
THE SPRING BOOK	Troy Alexander	£2.25
THE DEEP FREEZE ADVENTURE COLOURING BOOK		£0.75

You'll find these and many more fun Hippo books at your local bookseller, or you can order them direct. Just send off to *Customer Services, Hippo Books, Westfield Road, Southam, Leamington Spa, Warwickshire CV33 0JH*, not forgetting to enclose a cheque or postal order for the price of the book(s) plus 30p per book for postage and packing.